Events of

News for every day of the year

The last cargo sailing ship on British waters, the Thames barge *Cambria*, goes out of service on 15 October 1970.

By Hugh Morrison

MONTPELIER PUBLISHING

Front cover (clockwise from left): Elvis Presley meets President Nixon. The crew of Apollo 13. Jimi Hendrix. The Range Rover.

Back cover (clockwise from top): US Vice-President Spiro Agnew. The last British half-crown coin. Prince Charles meets President Nixon. The ten-shilling note. Janis Joplin. The Ford Pinto.

Image credits: Eliot Landy, Clem Rutter, Archives New Zealand, George Grantham Bain Collection/Library of Congress, Warner Bros, Anefo, Ron Riccio, Ross Houswright, Skeensss, Charles O1, Elen Nivrae, Erich Koch, Gage Skidmore, Rob C Croes, Svenska Barnboksinstitutet, NASA, Joost Evers, Pedro Ximenez, Andrew Dixon/ Maksim, Jim Ross, Jean-Luc, Allen Watkin, Alan Light, Lane Family/ The Public Sky, Robert L Knudsen, Jack Hawes, Elektra Records, Carlton Reid, German Federal Archives, Andre Cross, D Chernov, Georges Biard, Mr O, Skip Taylor Productions/Liberty Records, Bembmv, Morven, Robert L Knudsen, Alan Warren, De Facto, Troxx, Andrey Shcherbakov, Solters Sabinson Roskin Agency, Szczebrzeszynski, Wire Photo, National General Pictures.

Published in Great Britain by Montpelier Publishing.
Printed and distributed by Amazon KDP.
ISBN: 9781072326243

January 1970

Thursday 1: The Ulster Defence Regiment, the largest infantry regiment in the British army, is formed. Consisting mostly of part time volunteers, it is the only British regiment to have been on continuous active service throughout its existence.

The age of majority for most legal purposes is reduced in the United Kingdom from 21 to 18.

The Half Crown coin (2/6 or 12.5 new pence) ceases to be legal tender in the UK.

Friday 2: Seven US soldiers are killed and eleven wounded in a Viet Cong attack in Duc Pho, Vietnam; the communists are reported to be increasing the use of heavy artillery.

Saturday 3: *Raindrops Keep Falling on my Head*, written by Hal David and Burt Bacharach and sung by BJ Thomas (as featured in the film *Butch Cassidy and the Sundance Kid*) reaches number one in the USA.

Jon Pertwee makes his first appearance as the third Dr Who on BBC TV in *Spearhead from Space*; it is also the first episode of the series to be broadcast in colour.

Sunday 4: The Beatles' last recording session as a group takes place at EMI studios in Abbey Road, London.

Jon Pertwee *(above)* is the new Doctor Who.

January 1970

Monday 5: The long running US soap opera *All My Children* is first broadcast on ABC-TV.

Tuesday 6: Australia's Johnny Famechon retains the World Featherweight boxing title after knocking out Masahiko 'Fighting' Harada in Tokyo.

Wednesday 7: Farmer Max Yasgur is sued by neighbours for damage caused to their properties after he rented out his farm to the organisers of the legendary Woodstock music festival in 1969.

Harada: KO'd by Famechon.

Thursday 8: French singer and Moulin Rouge performer Georges Guibourg dies aged 78.

Friday 9: Comedian Larry Fine, better known as 'Larry' in the Three Stooges, suffers a major stroke which ends his film career.

Saturday 10: The first building in Walt Disney World, the Preview Center, opens to the public.

Sunday 11: Irish nationalist party Sinn Féin splits between those who want to take political office and those who refuse to, (known as 'abstentionists').

Above right: **Ruth Warwick as Phoebe Tyler in** *All My Children.* ***Right:* Larry Fine of The Three Stooges.**

January 1970

Above: **Aviation pioneer Blanche Scott in 1910.**

Monday 12: Pioneering US woman aviator Blanche 'Betty' Scott dies aged 84. Known as 'the tomboy of the air' she is thought to be the first woman to fly an aeroplane in the USA.

Tuesday 13: The Nigerian Civil War (the Biafran war) unofficially ends as the commander in chief of Biafra's army, Colonel Odumegwu Ojukwu, flees into exile.

Wednesday 14: Civilian police (Royal Ulster Constabulary) officers begin to patrol the Falls Road area of Belfast, Northern Ireland, for the first time since British troops were sent in to maintain order in August 1969.

Thursday 15: After nearly three years of conflict with Nigeria, secessionist Biafran forces under Phillip Effiong formally surrender.

Friday 16: Colonel Muammar Gaddafi is proclaimed head of state of Libya.

Saturday 17: *Sporting News* names Willy Mays as Baseball Player of the Decade for the 1960s.

Muammar Gaddafi.

Sunday 18: Swedish skater Hasse Börjes sets a world speed record of 500 metres in 38.9 seconds.

January 1970

Monday 19: US TV personality Hal March, host of *The $64,000 Question* dies aged 49.

Tuesday 20: The Greater London Council announces its plans for the giant Thames Barrier flood defence system at Woolwich (completed in 1981).

Wednesday 21: Five RNLI lifeboatmen are killed when the lifeboat *Duchess of Kent* capsizes during a rescue operation off the coast at Fraserburgh, Scotland.

Thursday 22: Pan American Airways begins the first scheduled Boeing 747 'jumbo jet' service from New York to London.

Friday 23: The TIROS-M (ITOS-1) weather satellite is launched in the USA.

Artist's impression of the TIROS-M satellite in orbit.

Saturday 24: Caresse Crosby, designer of the first patented modern brassiere, dies aged 78.

Sunday 25: Robert Altman's comedy film about the Korean War, *M*A*S*H,* is released.

January/February 1970

Monday 26: Mick Jagger of the Rolling Stones is fined £200 for possession of cannabis.

Tuesday 27: Beatles drummer Ringo Starr makes a special guest appearance on US comedy TV series, *Rowan and Martin's Laugh-In*.

Wednesday 28: Lubomír Strougal becomes Prime Minister of Czechoslovakia.

Thursday 29: The USSR performs a nuclear test at Eastern Kazakh/Semipalitinsk.

Friday 30: The last racially segregated schools in the southern USA close, reopening on Monday with full integration.

Saturday 31: Actress and singer Minnie Driver (*Good Will Hunting*) is born in London, England.

Members of cult hippy band The Grateful Dead *(above)* are arrested for possession of LSD.

Sunday 1: 236 people are killed in the worst rail accident in south America's history, when two trains collide at Benavidez near Buenos Aires, Argentina.

February 1970

Monday 2: John Wayne wins a Golden Globe award for his performance as Rooster Cogburn in the 1969 western *True Grit*.

Veteran British philosopher and pacifist Bertrand Russell dies aged 97.

Tuesday 3: Diminutive actor Warwick Davis (*Willow, Star Wars Episode VI, Harry Potter*), founder of the Reduced Height Theatre Company, is born in Epsom, Surrey, England.

Bertrand Russell.

Wednesday 4: *Patton*, the Academy Award-winning biopic of Second World War commander General George S Patton, starring George C Scott, premieres in New York City.

Thursday 5: Baseball star Rudy York (Detroit Tigers, Boston Red Sox) dies aged 56.

Friday 6: Prolific US actor Roscoe Karns (*It Happened One Night, His Girl Friday*) dies aged 78.

Warwick Davis.

Saturday 7: The US figure skating championships are won by Janet Lynn and Tim Wood.

Sunday 8: *M*A*S*H* reaches number one in the US cinema box office rankings, with overall takings of nearly $5m.

February 1970

Monday 9: The song *Thank You* by Sly and the Family Stone is certified gold after selling 500,000 copies.

Tuesday 10: 41 people are killed during an avalanche at Val-d'Isère, France.

Wednesday 11: Japan launches its first satellite, Ohsumi.

Thursday 12: Anthony Shaffer's long running play *Sleuth* premieres on Broadway. It is later made into a film starring Michael Caine and Laurence Olivier.

Friday 13: *Black Sabbath*, widely regarded as the first heavy metal album, is released by rock group Black Sabbath *(left)*.

Saturday 14: British Actor Simon Pegg *(left)* (*Spaced, Shaun of the Dead, Hot Fuzz*) is born in Brockworth, Gloucestershire.

Sunday 15: 102 people are killed when a DC-9 airliner crashes shortly after take off at Santo Domingo in the Dominican Republic.

Popular children's serial *Catweazle*, starring Geoffrey Bayldon, is first broadcast on British TV.

Hugh Dowding, commander of RAF Fighter Command during the Battle of Britain, dies aged 87.

February 1970

Monday 16: Joe Frazier wins the boxing heavyweight title after knocking out Jimmy Ellis after five rounds in Madison Square Garden, New York City.

Tuesday 17: US Army officer and doctor Jeffrey R MacDonald kills his pregnant wife and two daughters at Fort Bragg, North Carolina. MacDonald blames the crime on a gang of hippies, but is eventually convicted in 1979.

Wednesday 18: A jury finds the 'Chicago Seven' group of anti-war protestors not guilty of incitement to riot following disruptions at the 1968 Democratic Convention in Chicago, Illinois.

Thursday 19: The Poseidon Bubble reaches its peak. Shares in Australian nickel mining company Poseidon NL reach a price of approximately $280 per share then crash; the company goes into administration in 1974.

Friday 20: French composer Andre Louis Wolff (*L'Oiseau Bleu*) dies aged 85.

Saturday 21: Construction begins on the Boğaziçi suspension bridge over the Bosphorus straits in Istanbul, Turkey.

Sunday 22: Pete Hamilton wins the Daytona 500 motor race in Daytona Beach, Florida in a Plymouth Superbird.

Pete Hamilton with his Plymouth Superbird.

February/March 1970

Monday 23: Guyana becomes a republic within the British Commonwealth.

Tuesday 24: 29 Swiss Army officers are killed during an avalanche in Reckingen, Switzerland.

Portrait of Mark Rothko, by Denisova Olesya Alexandrovna.

Wednesday 25: American abstract expressionist artist Mark Rothko dies aged 66.

Thursday 26: The Beatles release their album *Hey Jude*, originally titled *The Beatles Again*.

Friday 27: Scottish author, diplomat and secret agent Sir Robert Bruce Lockhart dies aged 82. His memoirs were made into the 1932 film *British Agent* starring Leslie Howard and Kay Francis and were also the inspiration for the TV series *Reilly, Ace of Spies*.

Saturday 28: Caroline Walker sets the world marathon record for a woman at 3.02.53 at Seaside, Oregon.

Sunday 1: The USA ends commercial whale hunting.

Right: poster for the 1932 film *British Agent*.

March 1970

Monday 2: Rhodesia declares itself a republic, breaking its last links with Great Britain.

Tuesday 3: Australian tennis star Kristine Kunce is born in Sydney, New South Wales.

Wednesday 4: All 57 crew members are killed when the French submarine *Eurydice* explodes in the Mediterranean Sea; the cause of the disaster is never established.

Thursday 5: The Nuclear Non-Proliferation Treaty, intended to stop the spread of nuclear weapons worldwide, goes into effect.

Friday 6: The Beatles release their single *Let it Be* in the UK.

Left: Rachel Weisz, born 7 March.

The Citroen SM.

Saturday 7: French motor company Citroen launches the high performance SM car.

Actress Rachel Weisz (*The Mummy*, *About a Boy*) is born in London, England.

Sunday 8: 167 patrons and staff are arrested during a police raid on the Snake Pit gay bar in Greenwich Village, New York.

March 1970

Monday 9: The US and Mexican governments announce a pact to fight drug trafficking; the USA pledges $1m to help destroy marijuana crops in Mexico.

Tuesday 10: In scenes reminiscent of the 1949 comedy film *Passport to Pimlico*, protestors declare east London's Isle of Dogs district an independent republic. Led by local lighterman Ted Johns, the rebels block the roads into the district in protest over a lack of council investment. The area later receives substantial government money, eventually becoming the epicentre of the capital's financial services boom in the 1980s.

Fifth Dimension.

Wednesday 11: *Aquarius/Let the Sunshine In* by Fifth Dimension from the musical *Hair* wins Record of the Year in the 12th Grammy Awards.

Mystery writer Erle Stanley Gardner, creator of Perry Mason, dies aged 80.

Thursday 12: 18-20 year olds in the UK vote for the first time, in the Bridgwater by-election.

Friday 13: San Francisco city employees begin a four-day strike.

Saturday 14: The *New York Times* announces figures showing an unparalled level of racial integration in southern schools.

Sunday 15: The Expo '70 World's Fair opens in Osaka, Japan. It is the first world's fair to be held in the country.

March 1970

The NEB.

Monday 16: The New English Bible (NEB), a new translation using modern language, is completed.

Tuesday 17: The US army charges 14 officers in connection with the massacre of civilians at My Lai in Vietnam in 1968.

Wednesday 18: A two-week long nationwide US postal strike begins; troops are sent in to New York City post offices to handle mail.

Thursday 19: East and West German leaders meet in East Germany; according to some reports, crowds shouting pro-western slogans are pushed back by police and replaced with those shouting communist slogans.

Friday 20: 20 people are killed in an arson attack on the Ozark Hotel in Seattle, Washington; the perpetrator is never identified.

Saturday 21: The Republic of Ireland wins the Eurovision Song Contest with *All Kinds of Everything* by Dana.

Sunday 22: North Vietnamese and Laotian forces clash at Long Tieng.

Dana sings the winning entry in the 1970 Eurovision Song Contest.

March 1970

Monday 23: 18 victims of the Thalidomide drug which caused birth defects in unborn children are awarded compensation totalling £370,000 by England's High Court.

Tuesday 24: The US Coastguard Academy expels nine cadets for marijuana possession and use; they are the first drug related expulsions in the college's history.

Concorde.

Wednesday 25: The Anglo-French supersonic jet liner *Concorde* makes its first supersonic flight (Mach 1).

Thursday 26: Peter Yarrow of the pop trio Peter Paul and Mary is convicted of 'taking improper liberties' with a 14 year old female fan in his hotel room. He receives a Presidential Pardon for the offence in 1981.

Friday 27: Beatles drummer Ringo Starr releases his first solo album, *Sentimental Journey.*

Saturday 28: Over 1000 people die when an earthquake measuring 7.2 on the Richter scale hits the Gediz region of western Turkey.

Vince Vaughan.

Actor Vince Vaughan (*Swingers, Anchorman, Wedding Crashers*) is born in Minneapolis, Minnesota.

Sunday 29: Easter Sunday air travel in the USA is heavily disrupted by a walkout of federal air traffic controllers and a surprise snowstorm in the northeast.

March/April 1970

Prince Sihanouk of Cambodia.

Monday 30: Violent clashes take place in Cambodia between government troops and supporters of former head of state Prince Sihanouk, who was deposed on 18 March.

Tuesday 31: Japan Airlines Flight 351 travelling from Tokyo to Fukuoka is hijacked by members of the Japanese Red Army terrorist group. All hostages are eventually released and the hijackers flee to North Korea.

Wednesday 1: The Public Health Cigarette Smoking Act becomes law in the USA, prohibiting all TV and radio advertising of cigarettes from 1 January 1971. A similar ban in the UK went into effect in 1965.

Thursday 2: US Secretary of State William Rogers announces that there will be no US military involvement in Cambodia despite its recent upheavals and proximity to Vietnam.

Friday 3: Oil spillage becomes a federal crime in the USA; oil companies are made liable for all cleaning of spills.

Saturday 4: Members of the Soviet secret service, the KGB, exhume the bone fragments of Adolf Hitler, Eva Braun and members of the Goebbels family whose remains had been secretly buried in 1945. The fragments are pulverised and thrown into the Biederitz river.

Sunday 5: The Japan airlines flight captured by terrorists on 31 March returns to Tokyo after its hijackers claim asylum in North Korea.

April 1970

Monday 6: BBC Radio Four broadcasts the first edition of its long running news programme, *PM.*

Tuesday 7: *Midnight Cowboy*, starring Dustin Hoffman and Jon Voight, wins the Oscar for Best Picture in the 42nd Academy Awards.

Dustin Hoffman.

Wednesday 8: 46 children are killed when Israeli jets bomb a school at Bahr-el-Baqar near Port Said in Egypt. Israel claims they thought the school was a military base.

Tenggren's artwork for *Snow White*.

Thursday 9: Gustaf Tenggren, chief illustrator for Walt Disney features such as *Snow White and the Seven Dwarfs, Fantasia, Bambi* and *Pinocchio* dies aged 73.

Friday 10: Paul McCartney announces he has left the Beatles.

Saturday 11: Chelsea and Leeds United draw 2-2 in the FA Cup Final at Wembley Stadium in London, forcing a rematch on 29 April which Chelsea wins 2-1.

The Apollo 13 moon mission is launched.

Sunday 12: North Vietnamese troops open a heavy attack on a US Special Forces camp at Dak Pek.

April 1970

Monday 13: An oxygen tank in the Apollo 13 cockpit explodes, forcing the crew to abort their mission and return home despite dangerous shortages of food and water, and freezing temperatures caused by damage to the cabin.

Tuesday 14: Cambodian premier Lon Nol appeals for foreign aid as North Vietnamese Viet Cong forces begin to cross into Cambodia.

Wednesday 15: Libya's Colonel Gadaffi orders a 'green revolution' to increase the country's farming productivity towards self sufficiency.

Thursday 16: Reverend Ian Paisley enters politics when he wins a by-election at Bannside, Country Antrim, Northern Ireland.

Friday 17: Apollo 13 splashes down safely in the Pacific. The failed mission inspires the 1995 film *Apollo 13*.

Saturday 18: The British Leyland motor company announces that its popular but ageing Morris Minor car, in production since 1948, will be replaced in 1971 by the Morris Marina.

Sunday 19: The stage version of Brendan Behan's novel *Borstal Boy*, adapted by Frank McMahon, wins Best Play in the 24th Tony Awards.

US President Nixon with the crew of Apollo 13.

Monday 20: Britain's Ron Hill wins the 74th Boston Marathon with a record breaking time of 2.10.30.

Tuesday 21: Following a dispute with the government over wheat production, farmer Leonard Cassley declares his 29 square mile farm in Western Australia to be an independent 'micronation', the Principality of Hutt River. Although officially unrecognised, the state issues its own currency and passports.

Ron Hill.

Wednesday 22: The first Earth Day for ecological awareness is held in the USA.

Thursday 23: President Nixon announces the end of most deferments of the draft. Previously, students and fathers were able to postpone military service.

British Leyland announces the end of the iconic Morris Minor, in production since 1948.

Friday 24: The Gambia becomes a republic within the British Commonwealth.

Saturday 25: China's first satellite, Dong Fang Hong 1 is launched.

Sunday 26: The World Intellectual Property Organisation (WIPO), an UN agency for copyright protection, is formally established.

April/May 1970

Monday 27: Actor Tony Curtis (*Some Like it Hot, The Persuaders*), a prominent anti-smoking campaigner, is fined £50 in London for possession of marijuana.

Tuesday 28: Actor Ed Begley (*12 Angry Men*) dies aged 69.

Wednesday 29: David Webb scores the winning goal as Chelsea defeats Leeds 2-1 in the replay of the FA Cup Final at Old Trafford.

Thursday 30: President Nixon announces that US troops will invade neutral Cambodia to confront Viet Cong insurgents in border areas; Britain refuses to support the invasion.

Friday 1: Demonstrations are held in New Haven, Connecticut, during the trial of several members of the Black Panther racial activist group.

Courtroom sketch of Black Panthers defendant Bobby Seale.

Saturday 2: Diane Crump, the USA's first female jockey, becomes the first woman to compete in the Kentucky Derby.

Sunday 3: The Trans-Arabian pipeline carrying oil across the middle east is damaged in Syria, causing oil prices to skyrocket.

Charles Haughey: dismissed in gun-running scandal.

Monday 4: Four students at Kent State University, Ohio, are shot dead by National Guard troopers during a protest against the US invasion of Cambodia.

Tuesday 5: 438 colleges in the USA go on strike in protest against US involvement in Cambodia; thousands gather to protest in Washington, DC.

Wednesday 6: In what becomes known as the 'arms crisis', Republic of Ireland cabinet members Charles Haughey and Neil Blaney are dismissed over allegations of involvement in gun-running to Northern Ireland. Although cleared of wrong doing, their political reputations are seriously damaged.

Thursday 7: *The Long and Winding Road* becomes the last single to be released by the Beatles in the USA.

Friday 8: The Beatles release their 12th and final album, *Let it Be*.

Construction workers clash with anti-war protesters in New York City in what the media calls the Hard Hat Riot.

Saturday 9: 100,000 people gather in Washington, DC, to demonstrate against the Vietnam War.

Sunday 10: Pro-US sources in Cambodia claim that 4000 Viet Cong have been killed and that large amounts of their supplies have been seized, estimating it will take several months for them to recover.

May 1970

Monday 11: 26 people are killed when a tornado hits Lubbock, Kansas.

Tuesday 12: General Wladyslaw Anders, a senior commander of the Free Polish forces in the Second World War, dies in exile in London aged 77.

Wednesday 13: The Beatles' final film, *Let It Be,* is released in the USA. It includes footage of their last public appearance during an impromptu concert on the roof of Apple Records' headquarters in London.

Thursday 14: Convicted Red Army Faction terrorist Andreas Baader is broken out of prison in West Germany by his girlfriend Gudrun Ensslin; while on the run they form the infamous Baader-Meinhoff terror group.

Friday 15: Elizabeth Hoisington and Anna Mae Mays are announced as the first women in the US army to reach the rank of brigadier-general.

Saturday 16: Robert Altman's film *M*A*S*H* wins the Grand Prix at the 23rd Cannes Film Festival.

The papyrus boat *Ra II*.

Sunday 17: Norwegian explorer Thor Heyerdahl sets sail across the Atlantic ocean in *Ra II*, a replica of an ancient Egyptian papyrus boat.

May 1970

Monday 18: Britain's Prime Minister Harold Wilson calls a General Election for 18 June.

Tuesday 19: Future US Vice President and environmental campaigner Al Gore marries author Tipper Aitcheson at Washington National Cathedral.

Wednesday 20: British TV broadcaster Louis Theroux (*Louis Theroux's Weird Weekends*) is born in Singapore.

Louis Theroux.

Thursday 21: South Vietnam's Vice President Nguyen Cao Ky states that his forces will continue to fight in Cambodia regardless of US involvement.

Friday 22: A tour by the South African cricket team is cancelled after several Asian and African countries threaten to boycott the upcoming Commonwealth Games in protests.

Saturday 23: The Britannia Bridge *(left)* over the Menai Straits in north Wales, is badly damaged by fire started accidentally by a group of schoolboys.

Sunday 24: Drilling begins at the Kola Superdeep Borehole in the Soviet Union. The research project aims to dig as far as possible into the Earth's crust. By 1989 it digs the deepest artificial hole on Earth at that time (almost seven miles).

May 1970

Monday 25: US President Nixon starts a presidential commission to investigate the fatal shootings at Kent State University on 4 May.

The Tupolev *Tu-144*: Russia's answer to *Concorde*.

Tuesday 26: The Soviet Tupolev *Tu-144* becomes the first commercial aeroplane to travel faster than Mach 2 (over twice the speed of sound).

Wednesday 27: A British expedition led by Chris Bonington becomes the first to climb the south face of Annapurna in the Himalayas.

Thursday 28: Bobby Moore, captain of the England football team is detained by police in Bogota, Colombia, during the build up to the 1970 World Cup finals. Moore is accused of stealing a bracelet from a jewellery shop but is later cleared of any wrongdoing.

Friday 29: Nine members of a Japanese climbing team are killed by falling ice while attempting to scale Mount Everest.

Saturday 30: The US army changes its rules on hair: soldiers can no longer be forced to have their hair cut to below one inch in length, and moustaches and sideburns are permitted.

Sunday 31: As many as 70,000 people are thought to have been killed when a severe earthquake and landslide hits the Ancash region of Peru.

June 1970

Monday 1: The two-man Soviet spacecraft Soyuz 9 is launched in the USSR.

Tuesday 2: Four workmen are killed when Cleddau Bridge in Pembrokeshire, Wales, collapses during construction. The accident leads to tighter legislation for box girder bridges.

Ray Davies.

Wednesday 3: Ray Davies of the Kinks is forced to travel from London to New York to re-record the band's hit song *Lola* because of a reference in the lyrics to Coca-Cola. The BBC had refused to play the record due to strict rules on advertising; Davies changes it to 'cherry cola'.

Thursday 4: Tonga is granted independence from the United Kingdom.

Friday 5: CBS News confirms that its reporter in Cambodia, George Syvertsen, has been killed in a communist ambush; two of his colleagues are still missing, presumed killed.

Saturday 6: Margaret Court of Australia beats Helga Niessen of Germany 6-2 6-4 to win the French Open women's tennis championship. This is Court's fifth French Open title.

Left: Margaret Court.

Sunday 7: The Who become the first group to perform rock music (the 'rock opera' *Tommy*) at the Metropolitan Opera House in New York.

June 1970

Monday 8: Abraham Maslow, the American psychologist famous for his theory of the 'hierarchy of needs', dies aged 62.

Abraham Maslow and his 'Hierarchy of Needs'

Self-actualization — morality, creativity, spontaneity, problem solving, lack of prejudice, acceptance of facts

Esteem — self-esteem, confidence, achievement, respect of others, respect by others

Love/belonging — friendship, family, sexual intimacy

Safety — security of: body, employment, resources, morality, the family, health, property

Physiological — breathing, food, water, sex, sleep, homeostasis, excretion

Tuesday 9: Singer-songwriter Bob Dylan is awarded an honorary Doctorate of Music at Princeton University.

Wednesday 10: US Education Commissioner James Allen is fired from the Nixon government. He was the only senior official to have spoken out against the Vietnam war.

Thursday 11: Communist forces seize the Angkor Wat temple area of Cambodia.

Friday 12: The International Red Cross evacuates foreigners from Jordan following clashes between guerillas and government forces.

Saturday 13: British actor Laurence Olivier is made a Life Peer in the Queen's Birthday Honours list. He is the first actor to be made a Lord.

Sunday 14: England drops out of the FIFA World Cup after they lose 3-2 to Germany in the quarter finals in Mexico.

June 1970

Monday 15: A group of Soviet Jews attempt to hijack a plane in Leningrad to defect, but are intercepted by the KGB. The group's leaders, Mark Dymshits and Eduard Kuznetsov are sentenced to death.

Tuesday 16: The trial of Charles Manson *(right)* begins for a series of murders carried out in Los Angeles in 1969 involving his cult members, the 'Manson Family'.

SO VENTURA CAL
47 6 2 3
22 APR 1968

Charles Manson.

Wednesday 17: The bodies of two children are found buried in woodland near Waltham Abbey, Essex, England. They are believed to be Susan Blatchford (11) and Gary Hanlon (12) who disappeared in March. This becomes known as the 'babes in the wood' case.

Edward Heath.

Thursday 18: Britain's General Election takes place, the first in which 18-20 year olds are allowed to vote. Edward Heath's Conservative party is victorious.

Friday 19: The Patent Co-operation Treaty goes into effect, making the patent procedure subject to international law.

Saturday 20: South Vietnamese forces launch a new offensive in Cambodia with US air support, pushing back communist troops from border areas at Kompong Thom.

Sunday 21: Brazil wins the World Cup in Mexico, defeating Italy 4-1; Britain's Tony Jacklin wins the US Open Golf championship.

June 1970

Monday 22: The Methodist Church in Great Britain allows women to be ordained as ministers.

Tuesday 23: The film *Kelly's Heroes*, starring Clint Eastwood and Telly Savalas, is released in the USA.

Wednesday 24: The United States Senate repeals the Gulf of Tonkin Resolution of 1964, which permits the President to initiate military involvement without a formal declaration of war.

Thursday 25: With half the country under communist control, Cambodia announces a military call-up for all men aged 18 to 60.

Friday 26: Syrian and Israeli forces clash on the Golan Heights in the heaviest fighting seen in the region since the Arab-Israeli war of 1967.

Saturday 27: Three people are killed during rioting in Londonderry, Northern Ireland, over the imprisonment of socialist MP Bernadette Devlin for incitement to riot in 1969.

Sunday 28: US ground forces withdraw from Cambodia but continue to provide air support for the South Vietnamese there.

British Leyland launches the long running 4x4 Range Rover on 17 June.

June/July 1970

Monday 29: Protests take place in New York City on Italian-American Unity Day over allegations that the FBI unfairly targets Americans of Italian descent due to perceived links with organised crime.

Tuesday 30: Communists push further into Cambodia with forces now just six miles from the capital, Pnomh Penh.

USAF Bell helicopters in action over Cambodia.

Wednesday 1: Britain's Home Secretary Reginald Maudling visits Northern Ireland and famously pronounces it to be 'a bloody awful country'.

Thursday 2: Three school districts (in Florida, South Carolina and Texas) are given a 30-day ultimatum by the US government to abolish racial segregation or lose federal funding.

Friday 3: The French army detonates a 914 kiloton nuclear bomb on Mururoa Atoll in the Pacific.

Saturday 4: The long-running radio chart show *American Top 40* is first broadcast in the USA, hosted by Casey Kasem *(left),* also known as the voice of Shaggy in the cartoon series *Scooby Doo.*

Sunday 5: 109 people are killed when Air Canada flight 521 crashes at Toronto International Airport.

July 1970

Monday 6: California becomes the first state of the USA to introduce no-fault divorce, where divorce is granted automatically if both parties agree.

Tuesday 7: Allen Lane, founder of the Penguin Books publishing company that revolutionised British reading habits in the 1930s, dies aged 67.

Wednesday 8: Roy Jenkins becomes Deputy Leader of Britain's Labour Party.

Thursday 9: It is announced that US President Nixon has established the Environmental Protection Agency to consolidate anti-pollution efforts.

Friday 10: An American Roman Catholic bishop, James Walsh, is released by Chinese authorities after being in prison for 12 years. He is the last Western missionary to leave China since the communist takeover in 1949.

Saturday 11: The first tunnel under the Pyrenees is opened, linking France and Spain.

Top: Allen Lane, founder of Penguin Books. Below: Roy Jenkins.

Sunday 12: Jack Nicklaus defeats fellow American Doug Sanders to win the Open Golf Championship at St Andrew's.

July 1970

Monday 13: Lt Gen Leslie Groves, US Army, who directed the Manhattan Project to build America's first atom bomb, dies aged 73.

Tuesday 14: Five British speedway riders die when their team bus crashes while on tour in Lokeren, Belgium.

Wednesday 15: British dockers vote to go on strike; the following day the government announces a State of Emergency and troops are put on standby.

Thursday 16: The Commonwealth Games open in Edinburgh.

HRH Prince Charles meets President Nixon.

Friday 17: TRH Prince Charles and Princess Anne begin a US tour, visiting Washington, DC and meeting President Nixon.

Saturday 18: A crowd of 30,000 watches Karl Wallenda, 65, perform a 1/4 mile long high-wire walk across the Tallulah Gorge in Georgia.

Sunday 19: Belgium's Eddy Merckx wins the 57th Tour de France bicycle race. This is the latest in Monsieur Merckx's victories: already this year he has won the Paris-Roubaix, Paris-Nice and Giro d'Italia races.

July 1970

Monday 20: Britain's Chancellor of the Exchequer, Iain Macleod, dies suddenly while in office, aged 56.

Tuesday 21: The Aswan Dam over the River Nile in Egypt is completed after ten years in construction.

Wednesday 22: Five US helicopters are downed in South Vietnam.

Thursday 23: In the most violent incident in the British Parliament since the assassination of Prime Minister Spencer Percival in 1812, a man in the public gallery throws two cans of CS gas into the chamber during a debate. Several MPs are overcome and one is hospitalised. The attacker, James Roche, states that the attack is a reprisal for British military action in Belfast.

Karen and Richard Carpenter of The Carpenters.

Friday 24: The first US troops begin withdrawal from South Vietnam, in a pull-out which lasts until 1973.

Saturday 25: *(They Long to Be) Close to You* by The Carpenters reaches number one in the US charts.

Sunday 26: The all-nude theatrical revue *Oh! Calcutta!* opens at the Roundhouse Theatre in London. Initially investigated for obscenity but later cleared of any charges, the show is a huge success and runs for ten years.

July/August 1970

Monday 27: António de Oliveira Salazar, dictator of Portugal from 1932-1968, dies aged 81.

Tuesday 28: The US Army drops its accusations of a cover-up of the 1968 My Lai massacre of Vietnamese civilians by Colonel Robert Luper and Captain Kenneth Boatman.

Wednesday 29: The British composer and conductor Sir John Barbirolli dies aged 70.

Thursday 30: The British dock workers' strike is settled.

Friday 31: Black Tot Day: the Royal Navy ends the centuries-old tradition of issuing a quarter-pint daily ration of grog (rum and water) to sailors. The practice is ended by Parliament because of the need for higher efficiency at sea; the Royal Canadian Navy continues the ration until 1972.

Royal Canadian Navy sailors are issued the rum ration.

Saturday 1: In an effort to reduce air pollution, the Japanese capital of Tokyo imposes a ban on motor traffic on four of its main streets on Sundays and holidays.

Sunday 2: The British army uses its new non-lethal rubber bullets (also known as baton rounds) for the first time to disperse rioters in Belfast.

August 1970

Monday 3: Mrs Miriam Hargrave of Wakefield, Yorkshire, sets a British record by passing her driving test on the 40th attempt; she is unable to buy a car, however, having spent all her savings on driving lessons.

Jim Morrison, lead singer of the Doors, is arrested for being drunk and incapable.

Tuesday 4: Jim Morrison, troubled lead singer of The Doors, is arrested for drunkenness after being found passed out on a doorstep in Los Angeles.

Wednesday 5: Robert Kennedy Jr, son of the late US President John F Kennedy, is charged with possession of marijuana.

Thursday 6: Commemorative services are held in Japan on the 25th anniversary of the dropping of the atom bomb on Hiroshima; France marks the day with a nuclear test in the Pacific.

Friday 7: The first North American Computer Chess Championship is held in New York, and won by the Chess 3.0 program written by Larry Atkin and David Slate of Northwestern University. A later version, Chess 4.5, becomes in 1976 the first computer to beat a human at chess.

Saturday 8: Arab guerillas fire rockets at Israeli positions but in most places a recently declared temporary ceasefire is holding.

Sunday 9: Communist troops are reported to have reached the outskirts of the Cambodian capital, Pnomh Penh.

August 1970

Monday 10: Greece announces the release of 500 political prisoners.

Tuesday 11: Two officers of the Royal Ulster Constabulary are killed by a car bomb near Crosmaglen, County Armagh, Northern Ireland.

Wednesday 12: West German Chancellor Willy Brandt and Soviet Premier Alexei Kosygin sign a non-aggression pact, the Treaty of Moscow, which officially recognises the eastern borders of Germany which were reformed in 1945.

Alan Shearer.

Thursday 13: England football captain Alan Shearer is born in Gosforth, England.

Friday 14: The Vatican resumes diplomatic relations with Yugoslavia.

Saturday 15: Patricia Palinkas becomes the first (and only, until 2010) woman to play professional American football when she joins the Orlando Panthers (Atlantic Coast Football League).

Sunday 16: Memorial services are held in Gulfport, Mississippi, for the victims of 1969's Hurricane Camille, the worst storm ever to hit the US mainland. 1000 people in the area are still in temporary housing.

Willy Brandt of West Germany *(far left)* and Alexei Kosygin of the USSR.

August 1970

Monday 17: The Venera 7 probe is launched towards Venus by the Soviet Union. Designed to withstand pressures of up to 180 bar and temperatures of 1,076F (580C), it becomes the first spacecraft to transmit data from another planet.

Angela Davis.

Tuesday 18: Left-wing journalist and activist Angela Davis is placed on the FBI's 'Most Wanted' list for purchasing guns used in a court-room shoot-out in San Rafael, California.

Spiro Agnew.

Wednesday 19: Chinese persons in South Africa are re-classified as 'white' instead of 'black' under the country's racial segregation laws.

Thursday 20: US President Nixon receives a warm welcome on his state visit to Mexico, where he discusses the control of marijuana traffic.

Friday 21: Cambodian troops hold back the latest communist assault on the capital, Pnomh Penh, but are reported to be close to exhaustion.

Saturday 22: US Vice President Spiro Agnew begins a tour of South Vietnam, Thailand, Taiwan and Korea.

Sunday 23: Actor River Phoenix (*Stand By Me*) is born in Madras, Oregon (died 1993).

River Phoenix.

August 1970

Above: Claudia Schiffer. Below: The Jackson Five.

Monday 24: Anti-war protestors bomb Sterling Hall at the University of Wisconsin-Madison.

Tuesday 25: Supermodel Claudia Schiffer is born in Rheinbach, Germany.

Wednesday 26: The Isle of Wight festival begins on the Isle of Wight, off England's south coast. It remains the largest music festival of all time, with an estimated 600,000 people attending. Acts include Jimi Hendrix, The Who, The Doors and Emerson, Lake and Palmer.

Thursday 27: The Royal Shakespeare Company's modernist production of William Shakespeare's *A Midsummer Night's Dream*, directed by Peter Brook, opens in Stratford upon Avon, England. It is widely considered to have revolutionised the staging of Shakespeare.

Friday 28: The Jackson Five releases *I'll Be There* which becomes the Billboard Song of the Year 1970.

Saturday 29: 30,000 Mexican-Americans march in Los Angeles in protest against the Vietnam War known as the Chicano Moratorium. Four people are killed when the protest turns violent.

Sunday 30: Courts in South Korea rule that long hair on men is legal; previously, police had been administering haircuts by force to any man found with long hair.

August/September 1970

Monday 31: 80s singer Debbie Gibson (*Only In My Dreams*) is born in New York City.

Tuesday 1: An assassination attempt on King Hussein of Jordan sparks off the Black September crisis of conflict between the Jordanian army and the Palestinian Liberation Organisation.

Wednesday 2: NASA announces it has cut two planned moon missions in order to bring forward the Skylab project for a manned space station.

Thursday 3: Musician Alan Wilson, leader of the blues group Canned Heat, dies from a drug overdose aged 27.

Friday 4: IRA member Michael Kane, 35, is killed when a bomb he is planting in Belfast explodes prematurely.

Saturday 5: Formula One racing driver Jochen Rindt is killed in qualifying for the Italian Grand Prix. He becomes the first posthumous World Driving Champion.

Sunday 6: Four flights en route to New York are hijacked by Arab terrorists from the Popular Liberation Front. One attempt fails in London when the crew overpowers the hijackers.

Alan Wilson of Canned Heat (fourth from left) dies aged 27.

September 1970

Monday 7: Donald Boyles sets the record for the highest parachute jump from a bridge when he leaps from the 1,053 feet high Royal George Bridge in Colorado.

Tuesday 8: Physicist Percy Spencer of Newton, Massachussets, inventor of the microwave oven, dies aged 76.

Wednesday 9: Elvis Presley begins his first concert tour since 1958 with a concert at the Veterans' Memorial Coliseum in Phoenix, Arizona.

Thursday 10: General Motors in the USA launches the Chevrolet Vega subcompact car.

Friday 11: Ford launches the Pinto subcompact car, its rival to the Chevrolet Vega.

Saturday 12: The unmanned Soviet spacecraft Luna 16 is launched towards the moon.

Sunday 13: The first New York City marathon takes place, on a circuit in Central Park. It is won by Gary Muhrcke in 2.31.38; the event attracts only a handful of spectators.

The Chevrolet Vega (above left) and the Ford Pinto.

September 1970

Monday 14: Singer Stevie Wonder marries Rita Wright.

Tuesday 15: King Hussein of Jordan forms a military government with Muhammed Daoud as Prime Minister.

Jimi Hendrix.

Wednesday 16: A man is arrested in Grand Rapids, Michigan, for making threats to kill US Vice President Spiro Agnew while on a state visit. Mr Agnew is also heckled by protestors at Saginaw, Michigan.

Thursday 17: King Hussein of Jordan orders the expulsion of Palestinian Fedayeen militants from Jordan.

Luna 16.

Friday 18: Singer and guitarist Jimi Hendrix dies of a suspected drug overdose in London, aged 27.

Saturday 19: The first Glastonbury Festival is held at the farm of Michael Eavis in Somerset, England.

Sunday 20: The unmanned Soviet spacecraft Luna 16 lands on the moon and collects rock samples; it returns to earth on 24 September.

September 1970

Monday 21: One of the longest running prime time television programmes in the USA, *Monday Night Football*, is first broadcast on the ABC network.

Tuesday 22: Actor Rupert Penry-Jones (*Spooks, Whitechapel*) is born in London, England.

Wednesday 23: The search continues for the three crew members of the hot air balloon, *Free Life*, which went down in a storm off Newfoundland after attempting to cross the Atlantic on 20 September. The search is called off after 11 days with no trace of the crew found.

Thursday 24: The television sitcom adaptation of Neil Simon's 1967 film *The Odd Couple*, starring Tony Randall and Jack Klugman, is first shown on ABC-TV.

Friday 25: Erich Maria Remarque, German author of the classic First World War novel *All Quiet on the Western Front*, dies aged 72.

Saturday 26: The Laguna Fire begins in San Diego County, California, the third largest in the state's history to this date. It lasts until 4 October and causes over $200m in damage (at 1970 values).

Sunday 27: US President Richard Nixon begins a tour of Europe.

Left: Mr and Mrs Nixon meet Pope Paul VI in the Vatican.

September/October 1970

Monday 28: Gamal Abdel Nasser, President of Egypt since 1954, dies aged 52. He is replaced by Anwar Sadat.

Tuesday 29: Red Army Faction terrorists rob three banks in Berlin, stealing 200,000 Deutschmarks.

Wednesday 30: The New American Bible, the only version of the scriptures approved for use in Roman Catholic churches in the USA, is first published.

Thursday 1: Millions line the streets of Cairo for the funeral of President Gamal Abdel Nasser, who died on 28 September.

Pink Floyd.

Friday 2: Pink Floyd releases *Atom Heart Mother*, which becomes their first number one album.

Saturday 3: Tony Densham sets the British land speed record of 207.6 mph in the V8-engined dragster *Commuter* at Santa Pod Raceway, Sharnbrook, Northants.

Sunday 4: Singer Janis Joplin *(left)* dies from a drug overdose aged 27.

October 1970

Monday 5: British diplomat James Cross is kidnapped in Quebec, Canada, by marxist terror group FLQ.

America's Public Broadcasting Service (PBS) goes on the air.

Tuesday 6: Alfredo Orlando Candia, President of Bolivia, resigns and is replaced by General Rogelio Miranda who himself resigns soon afterwards, replaced by General Juan Jose Torres.

Wednesday 7: The International Pilots' Association demands the right to boycott airports that do not have anti-hijacking procedures in place, and asks for bullet-proof cockpit doors on passenger planes.

Aleksandr Solzhenitsyn.

Thursday 8: Soviet author Aleksandr Solzhenitsyn is awarded the Nobel Prize in Literature.

Friday 9: Prime Minister Norodom Sihanouk's toleration of communist Viet Cong forces in Cambodia is ended as his government is replaced by the pro-US Khmer Republic.

Saturday 10: Pierre Laporte, Minister of Labour, becomes the second FLQ kidnap victim in Canada, sparking what becomes known as the October Crisis.

Fiji is granted independence from the United Kingdom.

Sophia Loren.

Sunday 11: Actress Sophia Loren is threatened and her secretary assaulted when thieves break in to her hotel suite in New York City. The robbers escape with $700,000 worth of jewellery.

October 1970

Monday 12: Following an unsuccessful launch in 1969, British Leyland announces its improved version of the Austin Maxi, the first British 'hatchback'.

British Leyland's Austin Maxi; the first British hatchback.

Tuesday 13: The US Army's Chief of Staff, General William Westmoreland, announces his support for plans to end conscription and introduce a volunteer-only army by 1973.

Wednesday 14: The Chinese conduct a nuclear test at the Lop Nur salt lake.

Thursday 15: The last commercial cargo sailing vessel in British waters, the Thames barge *Cambria*, goes out of service. On the same day the last canal narrowboat freight service, between London and Atherstone in Warwickshire, ends.

Friday 16: As part of the ongoing 'October Crisis', Canada's Prime Minister Pierre Trudeau declares a state of emergency and invokes the War Measures Act, giving powers of arrest and internment to the military.

Saturday 17: Pierre Laporte, the Canadian politician kidnapped by FLQ terrorists on 10 October, is found dead in south Montreal. The FLQ claims it was an 'execution' but secret papers published in 2010 reveal Mr Laporte was killed by accident during a struggle.

Sunday 18: Actor Lee Marvin marries radio producer Pamela Feeley.

October 1970

Monday 19: British Petroleum discovers North Sea Oil.

Tuesday 20: The Soviet Union launches its Zond 8 lunar probe.

Wednesday 21: John T Scopes, the American school teacher prosecuted for teaching Darwin's Theory of Evolution in the 'Scopes Monkey Trial' of 1925, dies aged 70.

Thursday 22: Singer James Brown marries Deidre Jenkins in Barnwell, South Carolina.

Friday 23: Gary Gabelich sets the world land speed record at 650 mph in his racing car *Blue Flame* at Bonneville Salt Flats, Utah.

Saturday 24: Salvador Allende is elected as President of Chile; he is the world's first elected marxist leader.

Sunday 25: The wreck of the Confederate submarine *Hunley*, which sank in 1864, is found off the coast at Charleston, South Carolina. It is the first submarine in history to sink a ship in warfare.

The 650mph *Blue Flame*.

October/November 1970

Monday 26: Gary Trudeau's long running newspaper cartoon strip *Doonesbury* is launched in the USA.

The USA's Federal Trade Commission announces that the tar and nicotine content of all cigarettes will be listed in advertising.

Tuesday 27: The Soviet Union announces that the Zond 8 lunar probe has been successfully recovered in the Indian Ocean.

The lunar surface photographed by Zond 8.

Wednesday 28: A cholera outbreak takes place in Czechoslovakia causing neighbouring Hungary to close its border.

Thursday 29: The US government demands the release of two USAF generals being held by the Soviet Union following the crash-landing of their plane at Leninakan on 21 October; they are eventually released on 10 November.

Friday 30: Fighting grinds to a halt in Vietnam as severe monsoon weather causes large floods, leaving 293 dead and 200,000 homeless.

Saturday 31: Actor and director Dennis Hopper (*Easy Rider*) marries singer Michelle Phillips in Mexico.

Sunday 1: In a disaster that shocks France, 146 young people are killed in a fire at the Club Cinq-Sept nightclub near Saint-Laurent-du-Pont.

November 1970

Monday 2: The re-opening of SALT (Strategic Arms Limitation Talks) between the USA and USSR in Finland is announced.

Tuesday 3: In the US mid-term elections, Democrats have large gains. Future Democrat President Jimmy Carter is elected governor of Georgia and the Republican future president Ronald Reagan is re-elected governor of California.

Wednesday 4: A feral child, known only as 'Genie' is discovered by social workers in Los Angeles. The 13 year old girl had been kept prisoner by her mentally disturbed father since birth and had no speech or social skills; she becomes a *cause celebre* for psychological and linguistic researchers. Her father commits suicide on 20 November just before his trial for child abuse.

Emperor Haile Selassie.

Thursday 5: The death toll of US troops in Vietnam reaches its lowest level in five years as the 'Vietnamization' troop withdrawal continues.

Friday 6: Emperor Haile Selassie of Ethiopia, the world's longest-serving head of state, makes a state visit to Italy.

Saturday 7: Argentina's Carlos Monzon knocks out Italy's Nino Benvenuti in Rome to become the world middleweight boxing champion, a title he retains for seven years.

Sunday 8: British TV comedy series *The Goodies* is first broadcast on BBC2.

November 1970

General Charles de Gaulle.

Monday 9: Former President of France General Charles de Gaulle dies aged 79.

The Soviet Union launches the Luna 17 moon probe.

Tuesday 10: For the first time in five years, a week passes with no US combat fatalities in Vietnam.

Wednesday 11: US President Nixon and other world leaders attend the funeral of General de Gaulle in Paris.

Thursday 12: Cyclone Bhola hits East Pakistan (now Bangladesh). It remains the deadliest cyclone recorded, and one of the world's worst natural disasters; over 500,000 people are thought to have been killed by the storm and subsequent flooding. The catastrophe leads former Beatle George Harrison to organise the fundraising 'Concert for Bangladesh' in 1971.

Friday 13: Climbers Warren Harding and Dean Caldwell refuse a rescue attempt while stranded due to bad weather on El Capitan mountain in Yosemite National Park. The climb is completed seven days later.

Saturday 14: Southern Airways Flight 932 crashes in West Virginia, killing all 75 people on board including 42 members of the Marshall University football team.

Sunday 15: The US army announces tactical changes in Vietnam, including the adoption of guerilla methods learned from the Viet Cong, such as the use of booby traps.

Monday 16: The Lockheed L-1011 TriStar flies for the first time. It is the third wide-body jet liner to enter operation, after the Boeing 747 and McDonnell Douglas DC10.

Tuesday 17: The Soviet Union's remote controlled Lunokhod 1 lunar rover, part of the Luna 17 mission, lands on the moon.

The first 'Page Three Girl' (topless model) appears in Britain's *Sun* newspaper.

Wednesday 18: US President Richard Nixon asks Congress for $155m in military and other assistance to Cambodia.

Thursday 19: The National Guard is placed on alert in Greenville, South Carolina, after a shot is fired at a school bus in what is thought to be a racially motivated incident.

Friday 20: The Miss World 1970 beauty pageant in London, hosted by Bob Hope, is disrupted by Womens' Liberation protestors; a bomb is also found under a BBC van at the event.

The ten shilling or 'ten bob' (50p) note *(left)* ceases to be legal tender in the UK.

Saturday 21: Operation Ivory Coast: US forces raid the Son Tay prison camp near Hanoi in the hope of rescuing prisoners of war; none are found as they have all been moved to other camps.

Sunday 22: A mercenary force lands near Conakry, the capital of the former Portuguese colony of Guinea, in what appears to be an attempted coup d'etat against President Ahmed Sekou Toure. The coup is unsuccessful and the troops leave two days later; a UN investigation concludes they were of Portuguese origin.

November 1970

George Harrison.

Monday 23: George Harrison releases his single *My Sweet Lord* in the USA.

Tuesday 24: Joseph Farland, US Ambassador to East Pakistan (Bangladesh), helps deliver food parcels by helicopter to victims of the recent typhoon; a papal visit to the stricken region is also announced.

Wednesday 25: An attempted coup d'etat takes place in Japan led by anti-communist author and militia leader Yukio Mishima. The coup is unsuccessful and Mishima commits harikiri (ritual suicide).

Thursday 26: Pope Paul VI begins a tour of Asia.

Friday 27: Bolivian artist Benjamin Mendoza attempts to assassinate the Pope in Manila, Phillippines, as he meets President Ferdinand Marcos; the knife attack is foiled by the Pope's aide Pasquale Macchi.

Saturday 28: Montreal beats Calgary 23-10 in the Canadian Football Championship.

Pope Paul VI.

Sunday 29: England's cricket legend Colin Cowdrey becomes the most prolific Test batsman (7459 runs) in the First Test against Australia. The record is surpassed by Gary Sobers in 1972.

November/December 1970

Monday 30: Independent airline British Caledonian is founded.

A British Caledonian BAC 111 at Gatwick.

Tuesday 1: Luis Echeverría becomes president of Mexico.

Wednesday 2: The United States Environmental Protection Agency (EPA) is established.

Thursday 3: Canada's October Crisis comes to an end as kidnapped British diplomat James Cross is released unharmed by FLQ terrorists. In return, five members of FLQ are granted safe passage to Cuba.

Friday 4: Martial law is declared in Guipuzco, Spain, following strikes and demonstrations.

Saturday 5: Several people are injured and shock waves are felt in the New York metropolitan area as a series of explosions take place in an oil refinery in Linden, New Jersey.

Sunday 6: Police search the Las Vegas hotel suite of reclusive billionaire businessman Howard Hughes after concerns are raised about his disappearance. Rumours circulate that he has been killed and replaced with a double, or even a computer with a voice synthesiser. He is later found living in secrecy in the Bahamas. The incident is a partial inspiration for the 1972 James Bond film *Diamonds are Forever.*

December 1970

Memorial to the 'Warsaw Genuflection'.

Monday 7: During a visit to the Polish capital, West German chancellor Willy Brandt goes down on his knees in front of a memorial to the victims of the Warsaw ghetto in the Second World War; the incident becomes known as the 'Warsaw genuflection'.

Tuesday 8: Power cuts take place across the UK as electrical workers work to rule. Hospitals have to rely on army generators; in Kent, some hospitals are powered by a fleet of ice-cream vans.

Wednesday 9: The director of the US army's draft, Curtis Tarr, states that a move to a volunteer army is impossible while the conflict in Vietnam continues.

Thursday 10: Attempts to negotiate an exchange of POWs and a one month ceasefire proposal between US and North Vietnamese forces are unsuccessful.

Friday 11: The communist stranglehold on the Cambodian capital Pnomh Penh continues; petrol rationing is introduced as supply lines begin to break down. Anti-communist forces in the city, however, manage to hold out until 1975.

Saturday 12: NASA launches its SAS-A (Small Astronomical Satellite) Uhuru to measure x-ray data in orbit.

Sunday 13: *The Gingerbread Lady,* a straight play by comedy writer Neil Simon (*The Odd Couple*) opens on Broadway to mixed reviews.

December 1970

Monday 14: The electrical unions' work to rule strike in Britain comes to an end following public pressure.

Tuesday 15: The USSR's Venera 7 becomes the first spacecraft to successfully land on another planet (Venus) and transmit data.

Wednesday 16: The tearjerker film *Love Story*, starring Ryan O'Neal and Ali McGraw, is released in the USA.

Thursday 17: Polish workers go on strike in protest against high food prices; demonstrators are fired on by troops and martial law is imposed until 22 December.

Friday 18: The USA and USSR end the third round of the Strategic Arms Limitation Talks (SALT), agreeing to decrease the arms race.

Saturday 19: It is announced that 12 people were killed in the recent Polish food riots; the situation improves with news of the sacking of Communist Party chief Wladyslaw Gomulka the following day.

Sunday 20: Data on lunar soil from the Soviet Lunakod rover is received on Earth.

Ali McGraw and Ryan O'Neal star in *Love Story*

December 1970

The King meets the President: Nixon and Presley in the White House.

Monday 21: Elvis Presley meets President Richard Nixon at the White House. Presley discusses concerns over prescription drug misuse and offers his services as an undercover agent, which are declined. The meeting is kept secret until 1972.

Tuesday 22: Franz Stangl, the former commandant of the Nazi extermination camps at Sobibor and Treblinka is sentenced to life imprisonment.

Wednesday 23: The twin towers of the World Trade Center in New York City are topped out, making it the world's tallest building at 1,368 feet (417m).

Thursday 24: Walt Disney's animated feature *The Aristocats* is released in the USA.

Friday 25: US and South Vietnamese forces observe a 24 hour Christmas ceasefire. Thousands of troops sing *Silent Night* at the conclusion of Bob Hope's Christmas concert at Long Binh.

Saturday 26: *The New York Times* announces that doctors have found that violent behaviour in some people can be controlled by electrodes in the brain.

Sunday 27: *Hello Dolly!* Closes on Broadway after 2844 performances. The show ran for six years and won a record ten Tony Awards.